Step by Step

Helping parents and carers support young children's development

by
Dr Hannah Mortimer

A QEd Publication

Published in 2005

© Hannah Mortimer

ISBN 1 898873 44 5

All rights reserved. With the exception of pages 24, 25, 32, 33, 34, 41, 42 no part of this publication may be reproduced, stored in a retrieval system, or transmitted in any form or by any means, electronic, mechanical, photocopying, recording or otherwise, without the prior written permission of the publisher.

The right of Hannah Mortimer to be identified as Author of this work has been asserted by her in accordance with the Copyright, Designs and Patents Act 1988.

British Library Cataloguing
A catalogue record for this book is available from the British Library.

Published by QEd Publications, Trent Park, Eastern Avenue,
Lichfield, Staffs. WS13 6RR
Web site: www.qed.uk.com
Email: orders@qed.uk.com

Printed in the United Kingdom by Stowes (Stoke-on-Trent).

Contents

	Page
Introduction	5
The aim of the series	5
Sure Start	6
What is a Step by Step group?	7
What actually happens?	7
How to use this book	8
Chapter 1 – Why have a Step by Step group?	9
In theory ...	10
Playsense	11
Trackers	12
Which families benefit most from Step by Step?	12
Step by Step in Sure Start	14
Chapter 2 – Planning ahead	15
Informing colleagues	15
Planning rooms and resources	18
Inviting the families	18
Staffing	19
Planning your time	20
Booking crèche equipment	21
Selecting or designing your 'coat hanger'	21
Transport	21
Chapter 3 – Music time	22
Why music?	22
What you need	23
The right space	24
How to organise the music session	25
Close of session	30
Tips for music leaders	30
Target setting	31

Chapter 4 – Group discussion 35
   Starting points 35
   Week by week 36
   Different roles 38
   Rounding off 39

Chapter 5 – Evaluation 40
   Asking for feedback 40
   Attendance records 42
   Successful play tasks 42
   Reporting to management 43

References 44

Useful resources 44

Useful organisations 45

Introduction

The aim of the series

This series is for those working in Sure Start centres and other early years professionals who are planning to work with parents or carers of young children in groups. In recent years, there has been a blossoming of Sure Start schemes all over the country with massive recruitment and intensive staff training as more and more schemes come on line. Even after the first flush of schemes, there will be new and strengthened children's centres and community services that continue in their place. These books have been put together by practitioners who already have parent and carer groups up and running. They are the result of trying out approaches and evaluating their success. The hope is that they will provide practical ideas for colleagues starting new groups to prevent them having to reinvent the wheel. Inevitably, you will each be serving very individual communities with particular sets of needs, but it is hoped that you will find plenty of ideas in this series that will get you started.

Step by Step groups are a helpful way of working with parents or carers whose young children need extra support to encourage their development. Their development might be delayed in some sense (perhaps related to a condition such as Down's Syndrome), they might have other special needs or they might need extra stimulation and structure to make progress. The benefits of working in groups with parents or carers of young children are to promote friendship and mutual support, reduce isolation, and help adults share information and advice in a palatable and non-threatening manner.

Since the daily work of many Sure Start schemes is centred around family support and since this so often occurs in groups or 'drop-ins' held at a Sure Start base or community centre, these books are about how you make that delicate move from the informal 'drop-in' to the kind of structure that will enable you to improve confidences, relationships and quality of communications between parents or carers and their children under five.

The series includes books on:

RUMPUS Groups	behaviour management groups for parents or carers and their young children.
Step by Step Groups	groups that provide ideas and support to parents or carers to enable them to encourage their child's development (if the child is vulnerable or might have SEN).
Music and Play Groups	groups that provide circle time and structured play activities that improve relationships between parents or carers and their children.
Baby and Me	parent support groups that promote early development, relationships and communication in their babies.
Making Connections	therapeutic groups for parents or carers to help them form stronger attachments with their children.

Sure Start

In Sure Start schemes, families are targeted to receive information, support and guidance to help them make the most of their young child's developmental, learning and social potential, and also to improve upon their parenting and child-rearing skills. The aim is to improve the life chances of young children in areas of 'risk' through improving their access to education, health services, family support and advice on nurturing. Typical Sure Start schemes provide a range of services and provision – there might be outreach and home visiting, support to families, opportunities for quality play, learning and childcare experiences for young children and advice on child and family health and support for families who have a young child with special educational needs (SEN) or other disability. Even after the first rounds of funding for Sure Start, the aim is for the work to continue and to develop within local children's centres.

What is a Step by Step group?

These groups were based on the Portage home visiting scheme, borrowing from the step by step approach and helping adults within groups to support their children's development. Such groups have been running around the country since the first development of Portage in the late 1970s. The author was influenced by projects such as Knowlsey's in which parents met regularly in a local school or centre in order to learn new ways of teaching their children new skills and knowledge.

Each group has four to ten parents or carers who bring their children under five along with them on a weekly basis. They will usually have one child whose development has caused concern, though these groups can also run successfully with a whole group of parents who simply wish to understand more about their children's early learning and support them through it, step by step.

What actually happens?

As the families arrive, they move into a large playroom and sit down together on the floor in a large circle. There then follows a half-hour music session in which the children are helped to develop looking, listening and joining-in skills. Specific targets are worked on within the music session, while everyone shares in the fun together. After the end of the music session, toys are laid out for the children who play at one end of the room supported by crèche workers. They are free to stay with their parents or carers if they need to and to wander freely within the large room. At the same time, refreshments are served to everyone and the adults gather in a circle, sitting more comfortably on chairs. The group leaders help parents use a modified and simplified version of a Portage developmental checklist to plot their child's development and help them set learning targets for the next week to be worked on at home. Where possible, this links into a toy library resource so that toys and equipment can be loaned out to go with the teaching activity. The next week, progress is celebrated and next steps plotted. Towards the end of the session, everyone joins in a final 'goodbye' song and the group finishes.

How to use this book

You now have an overview of what a Step by Step group might look like. Here is an outline of what to expect in the book:

- In the first chapter, you will consider when and why you might like to run such a group and how it might fit into the Sure Start framework of provision, or indeed into the community service that you offer.

- Chapter 2 helps you plan ahead – what you need in terms of equipment, personnel, premises and skills.

- In Chapter 3 there are suggestions for the music makers group at the beginning of the session.

- In Chapter 4 there are suggestions for the group discussion during which step by step teaching targets are negotiated.

- Chapter 5 contains suggestions for evaluation and reporting back to management committees.

- Finally, there are some helpful resources and contacts listed at the back.

Chapter 1

Why have a Step by Step group?

In the first chapter we cover *when* and *why* you might like to run such a group and how it might fit into the Sure Start framework of provision, or indeed into the more general community service that you offer.

One of the prime reasons for developing Step by Step groups would be to pass skills on to parents and carers for encouraging the development of vulnerable children. Health visitors and Sure Start workers often identify a number of children whose development appears to be progressing slower than the average for their age or who were in need of greater stimulation and more positive and structured attention from the adults in their lives. These children might fall into two groups:

- Children who do not have a medical condition or have not been identified as having SEN, but nevertheless need their development boosting and encouraging. Perhaps the parents and carers feel a lack of confidence in helping their children and would welcome information and support as to how to 'help their children on'. For the sake of this book we will call this group a *Booster group*.

- Children who have already been identified as having a disability or other SEN and who would benefit from step by step teaching. The ideal provision for these children would usually be a Portage home-visiting service (see below). Groups like Step by Step should never be seen as a cheap alternative to a full Portage home-visiting service but can be a useful addition to this service. However, there are still areas where this kind of provision is not available or where you wish to start provision straight away while such a service is being planned and set up. The author has also run Step by Step groups from a child development centre, from a special school nursery and from a home group, where parents and carers themselves wanted to meet as a group and share their experiences and each other's company. For the sake of this book we will call this group an *Additional needs group*.

Because the second group is likely to include a wide range of developmental levels (including children with profound and multiple learning difficulties), you are likely to be using different checklists, such as the Portage developmental checklist (see page 44), and have a greater level of multidisciplinary input. One of your first decisions will be which kind of group you are going to run, depending on the level of need of the children and the other services available in your area.

In theory ...

What are the theoretical underpinnings of a Step by Step group? The approach is based on Portage principles which in turn are based on what we know about child development and also on the benefits of parent partnership. The Portage model of home-teaching recognises the primary role of the parent or carer and the importance of the home environment in the early education of young children with SEN. Within Portage, parents are partners in designing the education programme, teaching their young child with SEN and reviewing their progress. Moreover, it is an inextricable part of the Portage model that parents are represented on the Portage multidisciplinary management teams.

Portage was first introduced to this country in the late 1970s at a time when parents would have traditionally been taking their child along to a 'centre of excellence' for assessment, therapy and 'expert advice'. Parents found themselves having to relate to many different professionals and sometimes felt that quality input had to be specialist and professional if it was to have the best effect. Their own intimate knowledge of their child's needs was underused or undervalued and their role in teaching and supporting their children deskilled. The approach was developed initially in Portage, Wisconsin, USA, and brought together parents, professionals and families in an active partnership in the education of the young child with special needs. There are now Portage home-teaching services throughout the UK and beyond, many now based within Sure Start services. Registration and validation of training are co-ordinated by the National Portage Association (page 46).

The key elements of a Portage service are these:

- There is a regular (usually weekly) visit to the home by a trained home visitor.

- A shared assessment framework, usually the Portage checklist, is used which draws on the child's development to establish a profile of strengths and needs.

- There is a shared design, delivery and recording of a programme of teaching activities tailored to the needs of the individual child.

- There follows positive monitoring of the child's progress with regular reviews.

- A positive management framework draws on professionals from all relevant disciplines to support the delivery of teaching programmes and to resolve problems raised by families/members of the home-visiting team.

- There is regular evaluation of service delivery based on changes in the child's developmental profile together with parents' satisfaction with the service received.

- Management and advisory support for the service is provided by a team composed of representatives from all the contributing agencies and parents.

Additional needs groups run completely on Portage principles and it is essential that there are staff trained on the three-day Basic Portage Training Workshop involved in their running. Details of courses are available from the National Portage Association.

Playsense

There are many other schemes that have developed to support and strengthen the role of parents in educating their young children and these will be helpful for any 'Booster groups' you are running. One set of materials aimed at families of younger pre-school children is the 'Playsense' pack. The 'Playsense' materials are a guide and resource for parents and main carers who are interested in watching and developing the play of their babies and young children under three. They are published by the National Association of Toy and Leisure Libraries (see page 46 for details). A series of attractive colour-coded cards are organised into four broad areas of play and development: thinking and imaginative play; belonging and connecting; language play; and movement play. Within each area there are eight stepping stones representing common pathways of learning between birth and around 36 months of age. Each stepping stone card has a 'have you noticed?' section suggesting typical behaviour and ways of playing which parents might notice around each stage, though it is pointed out that each child has their own unique way of learning and growing. There are also suggestions for building on and encouraging play at around that stage. This approach fits well with the aims of the Association, since parents are encouraged to use and borrow toys and playthings at various stages to support them in their role as early years educators.

Trackers

'Booster groups' can also be built up around other checklists and tracking systems. The idea is that the checklist serves as a 'coat hanger' on which you can plot what a child can do now and decide reasonable next steps to work on. Some groups design their own checklist, perhaps modifying the Portage checklist and making it simpler. Others make use of existing systems such as the *Trackers 0–3*, *Trackers 3–5* or *Playladders* checklists, all available through QEd Publications (details on page 44).

Which families benefit most from Step by Step?

We have found that Step by Step groups are most effective for:

- children under five not yet in nursery or school;

- children about a year behind in any area of development;

- children who appear to be underachieving in their development, perhaps because of other problems or a need for greater stimulation;
- parents and carers who wish to meet in a group;
- parents and carers who would welcome ideas for helping their children develop and progress;
- parents and carers willing to work directly with their children at home.

We have *not* found Step by Step groups helpful for:
- a very diverse range of needs within one group (where some parents might feel discouraged at the speed at which other children are progressing);
- families who have been told to attend rather than who choose to;
- families who have not understood what is involved, i.e. that the activities have to be followed up at home;
- some (but not all) children with autistic spectrum difficulties who resist direct teaching. In such circumstances, we have tended to use other more specialist interventions such as those based on Hanen and Early Bird programmes (see page 45).

We have found Step by Step groups to be just as effective for children with all levels of disability or special need. However, the parents and carers we have worked with tell us they prefer to be with other families whose children have similar needs. While this is not always possible, we do our best to make each family feel individual and welcomed and to encourage families to celebrate their child's progress relative to where they started from rather than to make comparisons with how quickly other children might be learning. Most services, for example, make sure they are not using checklists with age ranges shown on them, since this can be most discouraging to some families whose children have severe developmental delay.

Step by Step in Sure Start

Here is an example of how Step by Step might fit into a Sure Start framework of provision. In Sure Start Stockton-on-Tees there are many schemes serving urban and diverse communities. When designing services for all, a framework of provision was set up in which parents or carers fell into three main categories:

- Hard-to-reach – they need support but may not ask for it or even want it.
- Mainstream – they both need and want support.
- Easy-to-reach – they probably do not really need support but want it anyway.

It was decided that, within the Sure Start philosophy, provision should be offered inclusively to all these categories and that it should be available at three stages of family life:

- Bump Club – prenatal support
- New Arrivals – early days of parenting
- Parent/carer and toddler – the pre-school years

This kind of thinking enables one to draw up a grid of support, making sure that each category of parent has access to support at different family life stages. Step by Step groups would fit into this kind of framework for supporting 'mainstream' families at the 'parent/carer and toddler' stage where there were concerns about the child's development. In other words, Step by Step sessions are helpful for parents or carers who want to support their child's development and who need structured advice and ideas about how to go about this.

Chapter 2

Planning ahead

Chapter 2 helps you plan ahead – what you need in terms of equipment, personnel, premises and skills. Suppose you have a cohort of several families that you would like to plan a Step by Step group for. This is what you need to do next.

Informing colleagues

You have a decision to make right at the beginning. Will you accept open referrals from any family who wishes to be included or will you only accept referrals from other professionals? The first would allow you to be utterly inclusive, but might lead to your providing a rather structured and staff-intensive resource for those who 'want it but may not need it'. Most children learn best through a balance of play, discovery and guided support from adults; they do not need the direct teaching that the Step by Step approach makes use of. You probably need some kind of system for identifying those children who, because of their learning difficulties or developmental delay, actually need help to acquire new play skills and learning – in other words, who do not pick up these steps incidentally and need a degree of direct teaching. If you opt for self-referral, you might also be missing those hard-to-reach families who would really benefit.

In practice, if your local service has developed to the point where a wide range of clients are already accessing your services and are well informed about what you have on offer and why, you might offer a combination of these approaches. Decide what your referral criteria will be and allow families to 'self-refer' on the understanding that you will then approach other professionals to make sure they meet your criteria.

To give you an idea of the sort of approaches you might make to other professional colleagues, here is an example. It is a copy of a letter to colleagues that one service decided to send out before starting their Step by Step group.

Dear colleague

Step by Step

It has come to our attention that many of the families with children under five that we work with share similar difficulties. We have identified a number of families where one or more of the children is developing slowly — either because they have lacked stimulation or because they might have special educational needs or another disability. To meet this need we are hoping to set up a Step by Step group that will run on Portage lines. It will not replace our Portage home-visiting service which will continue to run. However, some of the children worked with in the group may also be referred on to the Portage service for home visits.

What it will involve

It will involve weekly attendance for at least two terms until the child goes into school or nursery.

Referral criteria

1. Child's age under five and not yet in school or nursery.
2. Concerns about one of the children's development.
3. Child's development at least approximately one year delayed in any area, as assessed by the health visitor.
4. Referrals in writing please to: (contact details)

If you wish to discuss families prior to referral, please do not hesitate to contact us.

Yours sincerely,

cc. Portage service, health visitors, social workers, Sure Start managers, early years education support team.

Here is an example of a flyer that was available in health centres and Sure Start settings as one way of making the services on offer transparent and accessible to all.

STEP BY STEP GROUP

We know that children develop quickest when they are feeling happy, confident and successful. Some of you might have concerns about your child's development and want ideas for supporting this. Some of you might have a child who has a medical condition or special need that means you need to provide extra help if they are to make progress.

This group will run for parents or carers and their children under five and provide ideas for supporting the children's development step-by-small-step.

Contact your local health visitor if you are interested in attending. They will then refer you to us with further information to make sure we are the best group to help you.

Where? New Town Family Centre
When? Wednesday mornings
Time? 09.30a.m. to 11.00a.m.

You need to attend sessions regularly to gain benefit. The sessions would usually end when your child goes into school or nursery.

For more information, contact: New Town Sure Start Office

Planning rooms and resources

You need a large carpeted playroom with a circle of chairs at one end. You also need toys and playthings at a suitable level for the children to enjoy and play with. An optional extra would be a toy library resource on the same sight or a visit from a mobile toy library (there are further details of toy libraries on page 46). Refreshment facilities should be available nearby, at a safe distance from the children. Finally, you need a box of simple musical instruments (see page 24).

Inviting the families

Once the group has been agreed, this is the kind of letter that services send out to prospective clients.

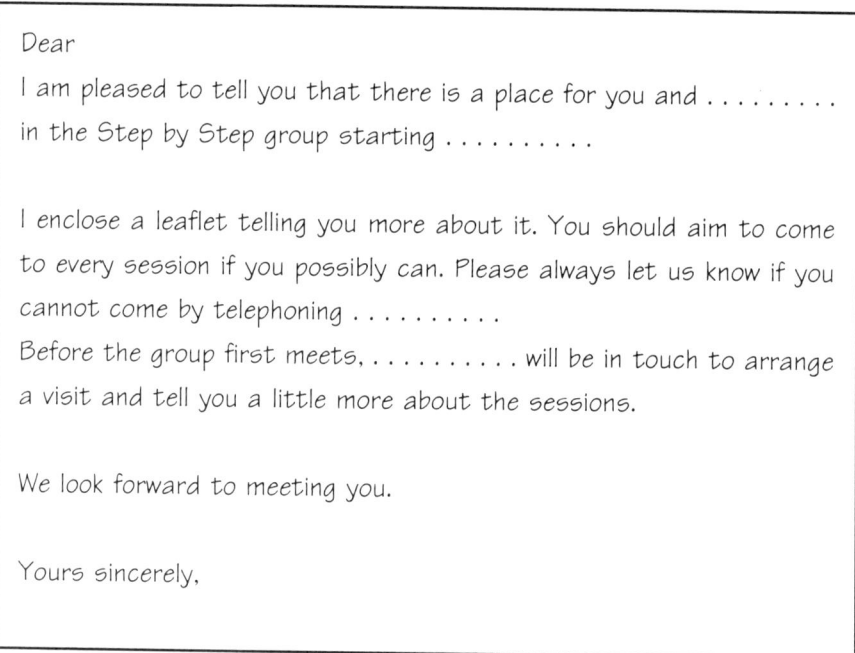

Dear

I am pleased to tell you that there is a place for you and . . . . in the Step by Step group starting . . . .

I enclose a leaflet telling you more about it. You should aim to come to every session if you possibly can. Please always let us know if you cannot come by telephoning . . . .

Before the group first meets, ... will be in touch to arrange a visit and tell you a little more about the sessions.

We look forward to meeting you.

Yours sincerely,

A follow-up visit or chat from someone who knows the family well is invaluable in moving the selection forward and reassuring or informing those who have been invited.

Staffing

Crèche workers

This will depend on how many children attend. Although the group is for parents and a particular child, there are likely to be other siblings not yet at school to be cared for. Once you know the numbers, you will need crèche workers to your usual ratios for the ages and stages involved. From four to ten families usually attend these groups.

Music leader

This person is likely also to be one of the professionals in the discussion group. He or she will need to have experience in promoting play with parents and young children in a group setting. One group used an educational psychologist who also had nursery teaching experience and was a musician. Another used an occupational therapist who had experience in play therapy. Another used a senior play facilitator. Confidence to lead and facilitate the group is as important as experience here.

Group workers

Whatever your type of group, *Booster* or *Additional needs* (see page 9), you will find it invaluable to have members of staff who are Portage trained and who understand the principles of target setting, long-term goal setting, task analysis and Step by Step teaching. For example, in the Stockton-on-Tees service, we arrange for all Sure Start professionals to attend a three-day basic Portage training workshop, ready for using a Step by Step approach or even developing their skills within the Portage home-visiting service. Once trained, these professionals will continue to need supervision and support. An excellent way of offering this is within a Step by Step group in which a Portage supervisor or psychologist also helps to lead the group. The ideal staffing is as follows.

Additional needs groups

- One senior Portage worker or psychologist trained and experienced in Portage.

- Two to three other Sure Start professionals (home visitors, teachers, early years practitioners) also trained in Portage (ratio one professional to three families).

- Occasional visits from other professionals involved with the children – physiotherapists, speech and language therapists, early years advisory teachers or occupational therapists. This makes sure your long-term goals 'fit' with what other professionals are hoping to achieve for the children and ensures team working.

Booster groups
- One senior Portage worker or psychologist trained and experienced in Portage.
- Two to three other Sure Start professionals (home visitors, teachers, play facilitators, early years practitioners) either trained in Portage or experienced in early years education and childcare (ratio one professional to three families).

Planning your time

To give you an idea of the timescale involved, below is an example of a timetable for the group.

Timetable	
9.00a.m.	Professionals arrive to plan and set up.
9.20a.m.	Families start to arrive.
9.30a.m.	Music makers group.
10.00a.m.	Refreshments and toys out.
10.10–10.55a.m.	Discussion group.
10.55a.m.	Goodbye song.
11.00a.m.	Families leave.
11.00–11.30a.m.	Professionals remain behind for planning and tidying up until about 11.30a.m.

Booking crèche equipment

Your service will already be familiar with the range of toys and facilities needed for providing a crèche and most Sure Start schemes will have a crèche co-ordinator who can assist you in this part of the planning. Take the trouble to find out a little bit about the children who will be attending and what their particular needs and interests are.

Selecting or designing your 'coat hanger'

Some kind of curriculum guide, developmental checklist or tracker is invaluable in helping you work out starting points and sensible targets for the children. In *Additional needs groups* you are likely to opt for a Portage checklist (page 44) or design a modified version of this. Because all the staff are Portage trained, they will be able to help parents and carers break steps down into even smaller steps individually tailored to their child's needs. In *Booster groups*, you might still use a modified version of the Portage checklist and you might find the Portage teaching cards a helpful resource, since the steps you will be working with will usually be larger than the tiny steps needed for children with additional needs. These are available from nferNelson (page 44). Reference has already been made to the 'Playsense' materials (page 12), *Trackers* and *Playladders* (page 44).

Transport

Depending on your location, you might find yourselves considering the need for additional transport arrangements for some of your families attending. Sometimes it might be possible to arrange for a family to join a special minibus service already arranged in connection with a crèche or other childcare service.

Chapter 3

Music time

In this chapter many suggestions are made for the music session at the beginning of the group. If you are familiar with other books in this series (such as *Music and Play* and *RUMPUS*), you will already be familiar with the use of a regular music circle time to get the group going, promote looking and listening skills, joining in and relationships. In a Step by Step group, the music makers session has the additional purpose of teaching developmental steps.

Why music?

Over the years, the author has found that professionals are horrified at the suggestion that they should start the session with a music time: 'We're not musical!' 'The families will be embarrassed!' 'The children won't sit still'. Time and time again, she has persuaded groups to 'have a go' and time and time again they have reported back that the music *makes all the difference.*

Music is an amazing thing – it stills a crying baby; it captures a toddler's attention; it holds the interest of children who, in any other situation, might be experiencing considerable behaviour or communication difficulties. It provides opportunities for even very young children to join together sociably in a group, long before they are old enough to attend an early years setting. Music encourages children who do not like to look and to listen to do just that. It provides a 'level playing field' for professionals and families to 'break the ice' together – after all, neither is the 'expert' and both will find themselves sharing a laugh or a grimace as the process does not go as expected! But most importantly, the children are *captivated* and sometimes, for the first time ever, parents or carers are seeing them look, listen and concentrate in a way they have never done before. This gives the parents a sense of pride and something to build on at home. It also allows parents to share pleasure with their children and allows the children to learn new steps without realising that they are 'working'. Above all, it is fun. As such a powerful tool, it is not surprising that music can be used very effectively to teach young children to learn and to develop.

The approach is based on *Music Makers* and you will find further information and suggestions for activities in *Music Makers: Music circle times to include everyone* by Mortimer (2005). The approach below is very similar to that in the other books in this series and so will be familiar to those of you who have read the other titles. This overlap is intentional – so that you can link your knowledge and skills from one kind of group that you run to another.

What you need

Start collecting or making musical instruments until you have a range of safe and attractive percussive and shaking instruments. A cassette recorder or CD player is also needed, unless you have someone who plays a lively musical instrument such as a keyboard, piano accordion or guitar. Make sure the quality of sound on the player is good, and have one adult on standby to manage the machine so that the music leader does not need to worry about it. We made our own CD with basic nursery rhymes and action songs and we all sang along to it. We did not simply 'let it run' in the same old order, but used it to back up the songs we had planned for that session. Aim to keep the music as live and individual as possible.

You will need a range of instruments that make a sound when shaken, when beaten or when scratched. Make sure they are safe for young children to handle and there are no loose parts that can be swallowed. Avoid blowing instruments which will need disinfecting each time they are used, unless the children bring their own. Make sure you have enough instruments for all the children and adults in the group. If you have a particularly popular instrument (usually the biggest drum), try to save up for more than one or help the children take turns fairly. We usually break 'band time' at least once to suggest to the children that they might like to choose a new instrument 'but only if you want to'.

Here is a possible shopping list if you are buying a set of percussion instruments. How many you buy will depend on the size of the group, but try to get a good range. You can opt for colourful plastic instruments or you can buy 'real' instruments which can have a better sound though are not so easily sucked, dropped or banged. Look for a range reflecting different ethnicity and which are safe for young children.

Instrument	Have	To buy
Drums to beat with sticks		
Drums to beat with hands, e.g. bongos		
Tambourines		
Jingle bells in rings and jingle bells on sticks		
Triangles – attach the beaters permanently with string		
Castanets		
Cabassa		
Guiro		
Wood blocks and beaters		
Indian bells		
Maracas and a selection of rattles		

If you decide to make your instruments, make sure beans and pulses are securely contained. Remember that some uncooked beans are poisonous and be wary of younger children swallowing loose, small parts or ingredients. You can make a range of sounds with dry pasta, rice, beans, sand, broken shell or gravel. You can make drums with saucepan lids or metal bowls with wooden spoons, and make use of large used coffee tins or upturned tubs which you can cover with bright paper or plastic.

The right space

You will also need a suitable area of your room to hold the music session in. Use a circle of cushions or carpet squares to signal to the families and children where to sit. The music leader should sit at the end of the circle nearest the wall so that the children are facing away from the rest of the play area. Keep the adults close together to form a simple barrier; this way, any toddlers are less inclined to run around the room. Alternatively, you can have a 'song carpet' in the centre of the ring for those children no longer on laps to sit on. Everyone in the room should join the music session (even the professionals who will be running the crèche session later) – the only exceptions are babies asleep in buggies!

How to organise the music session

One of you should be the music leader – depending on who is confident or musical. Use the session planning sheet below to help you plan the activities, aiming for 20 minutes' duration.

Step by Step Music Time	
Date: _____	
Activity	**Children's targets**
Hello song	
Action rhymes/songs	
Looking or listening games	
Band time	

Write in what you will do in each section and who will do it. This allows the whole session to flow smoothly. You should also write and share with other colleagues the targets for individual children. You should choose the songs and activities to meet the targets that you might have for the children involved (see page 29).

Warm up

First choose a well-known favourite to signal the beginning of a session and become your 'theme tune'. *The Wheels on the bus* involves actions and familiar words, is easy to pick up and seems to be liked by most children. Other favourites could be *Wind the bobbin up* or *If you're happy and you know it*. This should be your warm-up song at the beginning of *every* session. The warm-up song lets the children know that music is about to begin, makes them feel secure with its familiarity and immediately gives them an action to do in order to get going.

Hello song

You then need a greeting song to include and welcome all your families into music time. Make sure to include the names of any visiting siblings, toddlers or babies, even if they are sleeping. You should greet each child in the circle with a name, a look and a smile, perhaps a wave and a handshake or toe wiggle too. Ideally, you should encourage the children to look at you as you sing, and respond with a look, a smile or a wave.

We decided not to sing directly to the adults at first, making allowances for those who might feel shy or embarrassed. In time, we encouraged every single adult to join in the singing of this greeting song and we found that the older children joined in too. Never expect all the children or adults to join in singing all the songs. Both singing and doing actions at the same time are difficult for young children, but are much more likely if the adults are doing it too. The author has no qualms in sharing her embarrassment with the parents and families with a laugh and a plead, urging them to join in too if they possibly can. Just a few never do (or at least it takes several weeks) – the trick is for the music leader to carry on regardless, to show good humour at all times and not to add to anyone else's embarrassment.

Here is a simple version of a 'hello song', sung to the tune of *Tommy Thumb*.

> *Hello Daisy, Hello Daisy,* (move in and establish eye contact)
> *Where are you?*
> *Here I am, here I am!* (wave)
> *How do you do!* (take a hand or wiggle a toe)

Action rhymes/songs

Next move on to a few action songs or nursery rhymes. Keep the actions simple, starting with only one or two verses and building up until the children are familiar with the songs. Always try to have one well-known action rhyme and only introduce one new one in any one session. Encourage all the adults to model the actions and insist (with shared humour) that your fellow professionals do. Take the songs slowly to give everyone time to respond. Here are some ideas.

> *Old Macdonald had a farm*
> *Incy wincy spider climbed up the spout*
> *Two little birdies sitting on a wall*
> *Baa baa black sheep, have you any wool?*
> *Twinkle twinkle little star*
> *Wind the bobbin up*
> *Miss Polly had a dolly who was sick, sick, sick*
> *Humpty Dumpty sat on a wall*

You might find the books *Okki-tokki-unga: Action Songs for Children* (A & C Black), *Music Makers* (QEd Publications) and *This Little Puffin* (Puffin Books) helpful resources to get you going.

Looking or listening games

If children are to learn to listen and respond within their families, they will first need to develop their looking, listening and communication skills and to develop a positive relationship with their parents or carers. Here are some simple ideas of games that will promote these to start you off.

- *Tambourine shake* – shake a tambourine and encourage everyone to shake all over until you bang it to stop. Share humour and praise the children by name for looking, listening and stopping.

- *Where's the sound?* – ask certain parents or colleagues to shake or bang an instrument behind their backs and encourage all the children to look in that direction. Then ask the parent to reveal the instrument and all cheer.

- *Pass the bells* – pass bells around the circle making a big noise (this is a lovely activity for getting parents to help their children), then repeat for a quiet noise. End with a big noise again and cheer.

- *Who can use a loud voice?* – ask parents and carers to join in by replying, 'I can! I can!' in the right tone.

Who can use a loud voice?	I can! I can!
Who can use a quiet voice?	I can! I can!
Who can use a cross voice?	I can! I can!
Who can use a whiny voice?	I can! I can!
Who can use a happy voice?	I can! I can!

Band time

Place your box of instruments in the centre of the circle. Invite children to come and choose an instrument and ask them to choose one for the grown-ups as well. Start the tape or CD. Encourage everyone to play when the music plays and stop when it stops. Later on, you can have fun playing loud and soft or fast and slow as well. Praise children by name for looking, listening and stopping. Make sure that this is kept fun. Once the group has settled in, stand up and march round the room together (all of you) holding or shaking your instruments as you go. Children are fascinated by this and even the toddlers can join in independently and confidently. If at any point you feel that a child is opting out (for example by beginning to throw a tantrum or to cling), say, 'It's OK to watch too.' After a few sessions, once it is all familiar, they usually join in. Make sure you include all levels of mobility by carrying or using the child's buggy or rollator.

Finish

Announce 'Play time!' Ask for the instruments to be put back into the box and set the supported activity out immediately (this helps with the transfer from one activity to another). Sometimes, you can make a deliberate game out of placing the instruments *gently* or *quietly* into the box.

Step by Step Music Time	
Date: _____	
Activity	Children's targets
Warm up *Wheels on the bus*	Encourage Daniel to copy rolling hands. Encourage Daisy to wave. All can clap hands now.
Hello song *Hello . . . . . . Where are you?*	Sam to give brief eye contact. Daisy to wave. Kyle to respond to his name.
Action rhymes/songs *Incy wincy spider* *Jellyfish song* *Peter Rabbit* *Two little dickie birds* *Hickory Dickory Dock* (up to 4 o'clock)	Sam to allow his mum to crawl her fingers up his arm. Rest to copy 'out came the sun' movement. All shake to the tambourine sound. Daisy to make rabbit ears. Lee loves this – he can lead. All clap the hour – prompted if necessary.
Looking or listening game *Where's the sound?*	All to eye point.
Band time *Start and stop* *March*	Gemma to be supported with frame. Petie to step when supported from waist.

Close of session

After the play session (for the children) and group discussion (for the adults), come back together in the circle and finish with a 'goodbye' song, again naming each child and encouraging a look, a smile or a wave. You can invent your own or you can use this version, sung to the tune of *Twinkle twinkle little star*:

> *Now it's time to say goodbye*
> *Emily Thompson off you fly!*

Tips for music leaders

The success of the music session depends less on whether you can sing and more on how well you can 'hold the floor with gusto'. Holding everyone's attention, keeping a balance and maintaining a flow are all important. Everyone would quickly lose interest if you sat and sang songs for a full half-hour. By varying the presentation from quick to slow, song to chant, quiet song to loud song, you can keep a flow going. You will find you can hold attention for 15 minutes or so when you first get going, gradually building up to 20 or 30 minutes. Do not attempt longer at this age and stage. Use pauses to hold attention, stopping at key points of a song for others to join in (for example, 'One fell off, and then there were ...').

Use your own movements (approaching the children close or exaggerating the actions) to hold eyes and attention. Keep one or two surprises up your sleeve to renew interest, such as a puppet or props for songs such as *Five little speckled frogs*. Use the children's names and praise them individually in order to hold attention. Keep children with a short attention span next to a member of staff who can help parents or carers to focus their child's attention and demonstrate what to do to them directly. Try to keep this fun and non-confrontational. Make the children want to join in rather than tell them they ought to. If you really feel that you cannot sing (and this does improve with practice), then chant along to a musical tape and let others add the tunefulness. Children themselves do not sing in tune until they are about five, so you will not be on your own!

Target setting

Once the group has settled into a routine (after one or two weeks), you can begin to tighten up on your target setting for the children. Ask any crèche workers involved in the circle to observe one of the children and use the checklist on page 32 as a basis for this. The form should be shared with parents first so that they understand what is being done and why. They can also go through it afterwards adding their own comments or findings. The checklist is taken from *Music Makers: Music circle times to include everyone* by Mortimer (2005). Enter one tick for a skill that is emerging – that means that the child sometimes demonstrates it and sometimes does not. These are excellent starting points for setting targets. Enter two ticks if the child can definitely perform that skill and it needs no more teaching. That way, you can draw out skills to target for individual children and select activities that will be 'spot on' for that area of development. You will find much more detail and many activity ideas in the 'Music Makers' book. This kind of assessment allows you to carry out another observation at a later session and celebrate progress.

Music Makers

Name of child: _____ Group: _____

Name of observer: _____

In the Initial Assessment column – enter one tick if s/he can do that skill sometimes, and two ticks if s/he can do that skill almost always.

In the Target Skill column – tick skills you would really like her/him to learn in the music group during the next term.

Activity	Initial Assessment Date:	Target Skill	Final Assessment Date:
General			
1. Stops fretting during music			
2. Enjoys music			
3. Joins in group on parent's knee			
4. Begins to join in independently			
Listening			
1. Turns towards a sound			
2. Recognises familiar tunes			
3. Starts playing when leader does			
4. Stops playing when leader does			
5. Finds familiar voice from choice of two			
6. Imitates simple rhythm with prompt			
7. Plays loudly/quietly in imitation			
8. Plays quickly/slowly in imitation			
Looking			
1. Turns to look at person singing			
2. Turns from one sound to another			
3. Gives eye contact when greeted			
4. Looks towards a hidden sound			
5. Watches other children			
6. Looks at group leader occasionally			

Activity	Initial Assessment Date:	Target Skill	Final Assessment Date:
Singing & vocalising			
1. Makes general sounds to music			
2. Makes tuneful sounds to music			
3. Tries to sing familiar songs			
4. Joins in animal sounds			
5. Joins in repeated sounds, b - b etc.			
6. Joins in key words, e.g. 'down'			
7. Says familiar phrases, e.g. 'e - i - e - i- o'			
8. Counts to three			
Understanding			
1. Turns to his/her name			
2. Points to one or two body parts			
3. Points to several body parts			
4. Responds to up/down			
5. Responds to high/low			
6. Responds to loud/quiet			
7. Points to some named colours			
8. Shows me five fingers			
9. Understands 'look', 'listen'			
Actions			
1. Allows self to be prompted			
2. Demonstrates awareness of what comes next			
3. Claps hands to request			
4. Waves bye bye in imitation			
5. Joins in clapping song			
6. Moves hands for high/low			
7. Copies new actions			

Activity	Initial Assessment Date:	Target Skill	Final Assessment Date:
I: Instruments			
1. Holds a shaking instrument when placed in hand			
2. Can shake instrument			
3. Copies a hand beat on tambourine			
4. Holds two things at once			
5. Beats two parts of instrument together			
6. Beats drum with stick			
7. Blows instrument			
8. Joins in the band			
9. Plays fast/slow to different music			
10. Plays quiet/loud to different music			
11. Leads the band			
12. Marches and plays at same time			

Chapter 4

Group discussion

In this chapter there are suggestions for the group discussion time. This follows the music session and is a chance for the parents and carers to withdraw to one end of the room with refreshments as their children play with the crèche staff within their sight.

Starting points

When a parent or carer first joins the group, they are helped to complete a checklist (see page 21) in order to work out how far their child has already progressed and where a good starting point for teaching would be. Some groups would do this assessment as part of an introductory home visit (or several) before the group begins. If you decide to use the Portage checklist, you should have attended the basic Portage training workshop in order to understand how to do this kind of developmental assessment and how to use the information gathered. It is important (as far as possible) for the professional to actually see the child perform the skills before ticking them off. This is not so much a matter of 'not believing what people say' as making absolutely sure that a particular skill does not need further teaching. Some children will perform beautifully in one situation but not another. If so, we need to know this so that we can help the child feel confident to perform everywhere. Moreover, skills that are 'emerging' in this way make excellent starting points for teaching since the child can already perform them, at least sometimes. Usually parents and carers would hang on to the checklist, though you might wish to keep a copy.

Once an assessment has been made, the group worker and parents decide together on two or three sensible next steps for the child to work on over the next month or two. This is decided based on the worker's professional knowledge of how children develop and play and on the parent's expert knowledge of their own child and what makes him or her 'tick'. These 'next steps' become the 'long-term goals' to be worked towards over the next few weeks. The worker helps the parent or carer to break these down into easily manageable steps, starting with plenty of help and an easy task, moving step by step towards the more complex and independent. This is again where the Basic Portage Training Workshop comes in, since this approach is taught in great detail over the three days of training. The process of breaking down a long-term goal into easily manageable steps is called 'task analysis'.

Week by week

Once the initial assessment has been made and a series of steps agreed, the group provides the chance for parents and carers to come along and show what they have been working on each week ('borrowing' their child from the crèche where needed) and to negotiate with the professionals where to go next.

In the Portage approach, the worker always tries this out with the child first, and then the parent has a turn too until they have worked out together what to do. The idea is to end up with a simple little play-task that parents and carers can do each day with their child – about five to ten minutes of play – in order to encourage that tiny next step. This is written down simply for the parent and child to work on and record success.

In an *Additional needs group*, you are likely to be using the Portage activity chart that will be familiar to you from the Portage training. In a *Booster group*, you might decide to use a simpler version such as the Play Plan on page 37. The first sheet is written by the group worker. The other sheet (on the reverse side or beneath) allows parent or carer to record progress.

Play Plan for Billy

Target: Billy has indicated that he wants to manage his jacket all by himself

Getting started
Help Billy to pull his jacket off as far as the last sleeve, giving a tug at the cuff for him to pull the sleeve off. Give lots of praise and show him how pleased you are.

Games to play
1. Dressing up games: using old cardigans or loose-fitting items which Billy can easily take off himself. Use the mirror – he loves to admire himself!
2. Give Billy a chart to show how many times he took his jacket off himself. Add a sticker to it for each success. Billy has shown us that he loves stickers.
3. Allow Billy more time to manage it by himself.
4. Pull one sleeve over Billy's hand and say, 'Take your jacket off, Billy.' Remind him and encourage him until he manages, using hand-over-hand if you need to.

How to help
As Billy becomes more able, reduce the amount of help you give until he is managing to take his jacket off all by himself.

> **How did Billy get on?**
>
> **Monday**
> We got a new jacket for him from his cousin and it's a bit looser for him. He managed to pull off the last sleeve, but he still throws it on the floor!
>
> **Tuesday**
> Today Billy managed it all by himself, with only a little help to get started! I said he could go and watch TV as soon as his jacket was on the hook.
>
> **Wednesday**
> Billy loves the stickers! He had a tantrum when I wouldn't give him one straight away. What should I do?
>
> **Thursday**
> I noticed that Billy's arms are rather short and he does have difficulty reaching round the back of his jacket so I still help with that bit to stop him getting frustrated. No tantrum today!

Different roles

Usually the group leader circulates around all the parents and carers and the other workers work in a group of two or three families each. Once the group has settled down, you will find it very helpful to run the beginning and end of the group as a plenary session, celebrating successes and sharing ideas for support. Once the group is 'flying', you will find that the parents benefit greatly from what they can tell each other, with the professionals chipping in as necessary. When each group member (including the children) feels really settled and confident with the group, we sometimes end the session with parents or carers volunteering to show off a new skill to everyone. Perhaps their child has just learned how to put a jacket on or work a 'pop-up' toy. While parents and child show this off, everyone cheers and claps to the child's delight. While some children or families would hate this, others are really encouraged by the supportive audience. By this time, you will know the individuals in the group well enough to pitch your planning at just the right level for everyone.

Rounding off

Towards the end of the session, we announce 'tidy up time' and gather everyone together for a final 'goodbye' song. Play plans and checklists would normally be taken home by the parents so that they can try out activities through the week, as recommended by or negotiated with the adults running the group. These kinds of groups are usually open-ended. Families attend for as long as they wish until their child starts nursery or until it is felt (for example, at a multidisciplinary review meeting) that this kind of support is no longer needed.

Chapter 5

Evaluation

This chapter contains suggestions for evaluation and reporting back to management committees. You have several methods to choose from when evaluating an intervention such as Step by Step.

Evaluation studies of Portage have shown that parents welcomed the genuine partnership that developed in 'getting on with the job of teaching'. They also valued the fact that assessment and 'evidence' gathering under *The Special Educational Needs Code of Practice* (2001) was a positive and ongoing procedure and that they are celebrating and sharing their child's progress with a regular professional. As one Portage home visitor put it, 'As we enjoy the privilege of extended contact with the family, we share with the parents and carers a specialism in the child; his developmental progress, strengths and interests, personality and behaviours.'

Because observations and records are kept over many months, there is a genuine ongoing assessment to report as part of any statutory assessment procedure, overcoming the limitations of brief one-off assessments by unfamiliar professional visitors (or, perhaps more threatening, centre-based one-off assessments). Moreover, this ongoing assessment is carried out as a partnership between parents and professional, using a scale of reference which arises from the child's own strengths and abilities rather than a set of criteria which might be irrelevant to that particular child and serve only to pinpoint weaknesses. Parents are therefore strengthened in their role as educators and evaluators.

Asking for feedback

You might ask the parents or carers directly about what they thought about Step by Step once their sessions are over. Here is a form that you can adapt, using it either as a written questionnaire or a semi-structured interview.

Step by Step Evaluation

Confidential

Thank you for attending the group. We hope you found it helpful. Please give us some anonymous feedback to help us plan future groups – do feel free to be open with us.

Before the group began

How did you find out about the group?

Was the information given to you: Too much?   Just right?   Too little?

Did you feel prepared for the first session?   Yes   No

Coming to the group

Did your child enjoy coming?   Yes   No

Why?

What difference has the group made:

to you?

to your child/ren?

What changes in the group do you feel are needed?

What activity did you find most useful? (Please number 1 as most useful and 4 as least)

    Music time
    Playtime
    Step by Step teaching
    Other – please tell us what

Was the venue suitable?   Yes   No

Would you recommend the group to other families?   Yes   No

Why?

Thank you for your time.
From the Step by Step Team

Attendance records

One of the simplest ways to monitor success of the group is to keep a register of attendance (assuming that each family has enrolled to receive Sure Start services) or a tally count, week by week. Families soon vote with their feet if you are not fulfilling a need. In certain situations (such as a family's moving to a different group) this can be followed up by finding out why they no longer attend.

Successful play tasks

Another simple method of evaluation is to record the numbers of successful play tasks that were set for the family and achieved by the child by the next session. If you have completed the basic Portage training workshop, you will have learned how to write detailed activity charts week by week, setting a small play task for a carer and child to complete together. Integral to this is setting criteria by which you can measure your success – for example, 'Heidi will take a loaded spoon to her mouth with reminders and encouragement, three out of four mouthfuls' or 'George will match red cup to red saucer after watching Mum, four out of six times'. By teaching and rehearsing a small teaching task, say six times a day, it is possible to add this kind of measurement and to make a reasonable estimate of where a child's progress might be after a week of teaching. This enables you to look back and report that your activity chart was successful. This method works best if you set clear teaching targets that specify exactly what the child will be doing as a result of the teaching or intervention:

- *Who* (the child)
- Does *what* (in clear terms)
- *When* (under what conditions)
- To *what degree* of success

For example, 'Ali will climb down from the radiators when Mum calls him 50% of the time.' This is fully and usefully covered during the basic Portage training.

Reporting to management

It is helpful if you can report back to management regularly on the perceived effectiveness of the groups. One reason for this is to justify the staffing levels and resources. Unless you can show that the group actually promotes children's development, it might not be seen as 'value for money'. You will therefore find it helpful to report not only on parents' evaluations, but your own evaluations on how you feel those children have progressed and whether you have been able to reduce some of the barriers to their learning.

References

DfES (2001) (2001) *The Special Educational Needs Code of Practice.* Nottingham: DfES Publications.

Mortimer, H. (2000) *Playladders.* Lichfield: QEd Publications.

Mortimer, H. (2003) *Trackers 0–3.* Lichfield: QEd Publications.

Mortimer, H. (2003) *Trackers 3–5.* Lichfield: QEd Publications.

Mortimer, H. (2005) *Music Makers: Music circle times to include everyone.* Lichfield: QEd Publications.

Useful resources

Harrop, B., Friend, L. and Gadsby, D. (1975) *Okki-tokki-unga: Action Songs for Children.* London: A & C Black.

Matterson, E. (Ed) (2004) *This Little Puffin.* London: Puffin Books.

Pavelko, V. and Scott, L.B. (1976) *Apusskidu: Songs for Children.* London: A & C Black.

Music Education Supplies Ltd, 101 Banstead Road South, Sutton, Surrey SM2 5LH

nferNelson – you can obtain the specialist assessment catalogue for details of the Portage developmental checklists and the Portage activity cards.
nferNelson, Freepost LON 16507, Swindon SN2 8BR
Tel: 0845 602 1937
Website: www.nfer-nelson.co.uk

Step by Step (SBS) for colourful and more unusual musical instruments suitable for early years and SEN.
SBS, Lee Fold, Hyde, Cheshire SK14 4LL
Tel: 0845 3001089
Website: www.sbs-educational.co.uk

Useful organisations

Contact a Family, 209–211 City Road, London EC1V 1JN
Tel: 020 7608 8700   Fax: 020 7608 8701
Helpline: 0808 808 3555 or Textphone: 0808 808 3556
Freephone for parents and families (10a.m.–4p.m., Mon–Fri)
Email: info@cafamily.org.uk
Website: www.cafamily.org.uk
CaF directory of specific conditions and rare syndromes in children with their family support networks can be obtained.

Down's Syndrome Association, Langdon Down Centre, 2a Langdon Park, Teddington TW11 9PS
Tel: 0845 230 0372
Fax: 0845 230 0373
Email: info@downs-syndrome.org.uk
Website: www.downs-syndrome.org.uk

The Early Bird Programme – information from the National Autistic Society.
Website: www.nas.org.uk

Hanen Centre for parent training and publications.
Website: www.hanen.org/

Makaton Vocabulary Development Project, Firwood Drive, Camberley, Surrey GU15 3QD
Tel: 01276 61390   Fax: 01276 681368
Email: mvdp@makaton.org
Website: www.makaton.org/

Mencap, 123 Golden Lane, London EC1Y 0RT
Tel: 020 7454 0454   Fax: 020 7696 5540
Email: information@mencap.org.uk
Website: www.mencap.org.uk

The National Association of Toy and Leisure Libraries, 68 Churchway, London NW1 1LT
Tel: 020 7255 4600
Email: admin@playmatters.co.uk
Website: www.natll.org.uk
The National Autistic Society, 393 City Road, London EC1V 1NG
Tel: 020 7833 2299   Fax: 020 7833 9666
Email: nas@nas.org.uk
Website: www.nas.org.uk

National Portage Association, 127 Monks Dale, Yeovil, Somerset BA21 3JE
Email: info@portage.org.uk
Website: www.portage.org.uk

Scope, 6 Market Road, London N7 9PW
Tel: 020 7619 7100
Cerebral Palsy Helpline freephone: 0808 800 3333
Website: www.scope.org.uk